THE USPC

CONFORMATION

MOVEMENT

AND

SOUNDNESS

ALSO BY SUSAN E. HARRIS

Horsesmanship in Pictures

Grooming to Win, Second Edition

Horse Gaits, Balance and Movement

*The United States Pony Club Manual of Horsemanship:
Basics for Beginners/D Level*

*The United States Pony Club Manual of Horsemanship:
Intermediate Horsemanship/C Level*

*The United States Pony Club Manual of Horsemanship:
Advanced Horsemanship B/HA/A Levels*

The USPC Guide to Bandaging Your Horse

The USPC Guide to Longeing and Ground Training

THE USPC GUIDE TO

CONFORMATION, MOVEMENT

AND

SOUNDNESS

written and illustrated by

SUSAN E. HARRIS

RUTH RING HARVIE, USPC EDITOR

Howell Book House
New York

This book is not intended as a substitute for professional advice and guidance. A person should take part in the activities discussed in this book only under the supervision of a knowledgeable adult.

Copyright © 1997 by Susan E. Harris and The United States Pony Clubs, Inc.

Howell Book House
A Simon & Schuster Macmillan Company
1633 Broadway
New York, NY 10019

MACMILLAN is a registered trademark of Macmillan, Inc.

Library of Congress Cataloging-in-Publication Data

Harris, Susan E.
    The USPC guide to conformation, movement and soundness / written and illustrated by Susan E. Harris : Ruth Ring Harvie, USPC editor.
        p.   cm.
    ISBN 0-86705-639-7
    1. Horses—Conformation.   I. Harvie, Ruth Ring.   II. United States Pony Clubs.   III. Title.
SF279.H37   1997
636.1'08'1—dc21   97-3310
                                                                                        CIP

Manufactured in the United States of America

10 9 8 7 6 5 4 3

CONTENTS

About The United States Pony Clubs, Inc.   vii

Introduction   ix

   1. Basic Horse Anatomy   1

   2. Conformation   11

   3. Gaits and Movement   37

   4. Soundness, Blemishes, and Unsoundnesses   49

About the United States Pony Clubs, Inc.

The United States Pony Clubs, Inc. is an educational youth organization that teaches riding, mounted sports, and the care of horses and ponies, and develops in youth the characteristics of responsibility, sportsmanship, moral judgment, leadership, and self-confidence.

Since its beginning in Great Britain in 1928, Pony Club has become the largest junior equestrian group in the world, with more than 125,000 members in 27 countries. At this writing, the U.S. Pony Clubs have approximately 11,000 members in more than 500 clubs. Members ride mounts of all breeds and sizes, not just ponies; the term "pony" originally referred to any mount ridden by a young person.

The U.S. Pony Clubs teach a curriculum which covers balanced seat horsemanship on the flat, over fences, and in the open, along with safety, knowledge, and practical skills in horse care and management. The goal is to produce safe, happy, and confident horsepersons, who can ride, handle, and care for their horse and equipment competently at their level, with an understanding of the reasons for what they do.

Pony Clubbers progress at their own pace through a series of levels or ratings, from D (basic) through C (intermediate) to B, HA, and A (advanced). The requirements for each rating are called the USPC Standards of Proficiency. The lower level ratings (D-1 through C-2) are tested within the local Pony Club; the C-3 rating is tested at a Regional Testing; and the B, HA, and A levels are national ratings, requiring advanced levels of knowledge, horsemanship, and horse care and management skills.

Besides instruction and ratings, Pony Club offers activities such as Combined Training, Foxhunting, Dressage, Mounted Games, Show Jumping, Tetrathlon, and Vaulting, with emphasis on safety, teamwork, and good horsemanship and sportsmanship.

For more information about the U.S. Pony Clubs, please contact:

United States Pony Clubs, Inc.
The Kentucky Horse Park
Iron Works Pike
Lexington, KY 40511
(606) 254-PONY (7669)

INTRODUCTION

This book presents the basics of conformation, movement, and soundness, along with basic anatomy of the skeleton, foot, and lower leg. Conformation, soundness, and movement are important factors when selecting and evaluating horses and determining what type of work a horse is best suited to do. These are fundamental to a horse's ability to move efficiently, to do his job well, and to remain strong, sound, and able. Good conformation is always attractive, but desirable form must be based on function, not just on style or prettiness.

There are many different breeds and types of horses, bred to possess characteristics that make them suitable for certain purposes or disciplines. However, within a breed there may be several distinct types, and each individual horse is unique. The fact that a horse is of a particular breed (for instance, a warmblood or a Quarter Horse) does not necessarily mean that he will be good or not so good for a particular purpose or type of riding. Don't be "breed blind," either by a breed you admire or one you don't especially care for. Instead, judge each horse as an individual.

Regardless of breed, there are certain aspects of conformation, movement, and soundness that are important in order for a horse to remain sound. Knowing about functional conformation helps you focus on the most important points first: those which make a horse strong, efficient, and athletic (such as the shape and set of the legs), as opposed to merely stylish or pretty (such as the shape of the ears or the manner in which the tail is carried).

In order to understand conformation, it helps to know something about equine anatomy and the major structures of the horse's legs and feet. This also helps you identify and locate various unsoundnesses and understand what goes wrong when these are present.

In order to evaluate a horse, you need to understand the basic gaits and how horses move. This book will also help you recognize movement faults, especially those that can lead to lameness or unsoundness.

No horse is perfect; most horses have some conformation faults or blemishes, and some have serious flaws that compromise their soundness and performance. You must be able to spot defects and determine whether they are minor or major problems, and understand how they affect the horse's ability to do his job. Although perfect conformation and "clean," blemish-free legs are always desirable, some blemishes or old, healed conditions may be of minor importance. Others may indicate a serious weakness which could cause a breakdown under hard work or a chronic condition which may get worse over time.

This book will help you acquire a basic knowledge of conformation, move-ment, and soundness, but it is only a start. You will need to develop your "eye for a horse" by observing and evaluating as many different horses as possible. For further study of horse anatomy, movement, and conformation, you may wish to read *Horse Gaits, Balance and Movement* by Susan E. Harris (Howell Book House, 1993).

THE USPC GUIDE TO

CONFORMATION, MOVEMENT

AND

SOUNDNESS

CHAPTER 1

BASIC HORSE ANATOMY

To understand how your horse is built, how he moves, and what can go wrong with him, it helps to know some horse anatomy. Horses have basically the same bones and muscles as people do, although some of the bones and muscles of the horse have adapted into different shapes for different purposes. It is easier to understand horse anatomy if you compare each part of the horse with the same part of your own body. (It helps to remember that if you were a horse, you would be walking on all fours, on your middle toes and fingers.)

BONES AND JOINTS

Bones are the framework of the body. They support the horse, protect his organs, and act as levers to move him. Bones are held together by ligaments, which are strong, slightly elastic fibers.

A joint is a place where bones meet. Flexion (or bending) can only take place at a joint. Joints also absorb some shock.

The ligaments around a joint form a closed "joint capsule." Inside the joint capsule is a slippery oil called synovial fluid, which lubricates the joint. The ends of the bone are covered with cartilage, which is smooth and softer than bone. Cartilage helps to cushion the joint, absorb some shock, and let the bones move freely.

MUSCLES AND TENDONS

Muscles move the body. They are attached to the bones by tendons, which are like strong cables or straps. Muscles are made up of fibers which can contract (or shorten) and pull on the tendons to move the bones.

Parts of the horse.

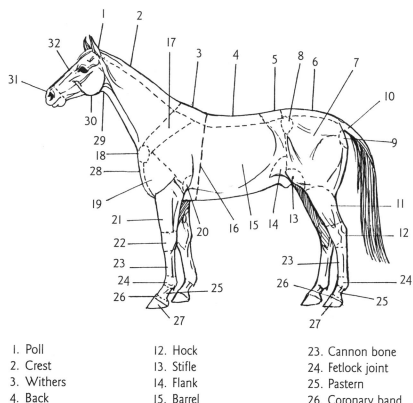

1. Poll	12. Hock	23. Cannon bone
2. Crest	13. Stifle	24. Fetlock joint
3. Withers	14. Flank	25. Pastern
4. Back	15. Barrel	26. Coronary band
5. Loins	16. Heart girth	27. Hoof
6. Croup	17. Shoulder	28. Chest
7. Hindquarters	18. Point of shoulder	29. Throatlash
8. Point of hip	19. Arm	30. Jowl
9. Point of buttock	20. Elbow	31. Muzzle
10. Dock	21. Forearm	32. Face
11. Gaskin	22. Knee	

Skeletal system.

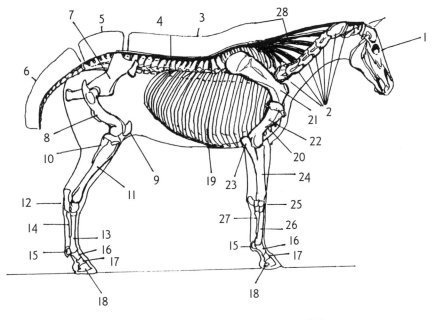

1. Skull
2. Cervical (neck) vertebrae (7)
3. Dorsal (back) vertebrae (18)
4. Lumbar (loin) vertebrae (6)
5. Sacral (croup) vertebrae (5)
6. Caudal (tail) vertebrae (18–23)
7. Pelvis
8. Femur (thigh bone)
9. Patella
10. Fibula
11. Tibia
12. Tarsal (hock) joint
13. Large metatarsal (cannon) bone
14. Small metatarsal (splint) bone
15. Sesamoid bones
16. 1st Phalanx (long pastern bone)
17. 2nd Phalanx (short pastern bone)
18. 3rd Phalanx (coffin bone)
19. Ribs (18 pairs)
20. Sternum (breastbone)
21. Scapula (shoulder blade)
22. Humerus (arm bone)
23. Ulna (elbow bone)
24. Radius (forearm bone)
25. Carpal (knee) joint
26. Large metacarpal (cannon) bone
27. Small metacarpal (splint) bone
28. Nuchal (cervical) ligament

Comparison of horse without human anatomy—major joints.

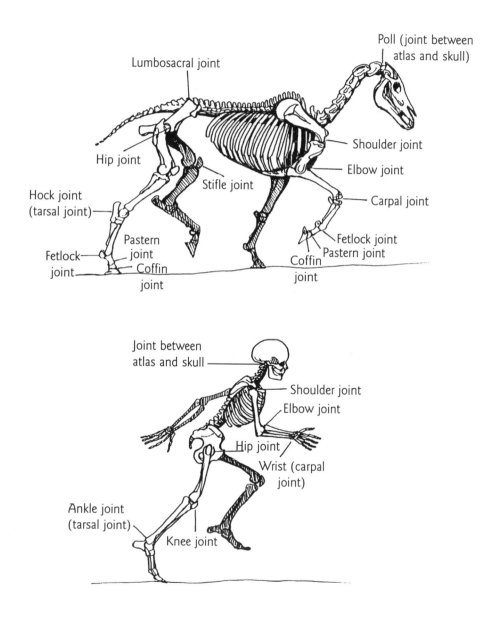

Because muscles can only pull, not push, they usually work in pairs. One muscle flexes (or bends) a joint; the other muscle extends (or straightens) it. The muscles and tendons which bend or flex a joint are called flexors; those which extend or straighten a joint are called extensors.

There are many layers of muscles in the horse's body—some close to the surface and some deep, next to the bones.

Skeletal muscles.

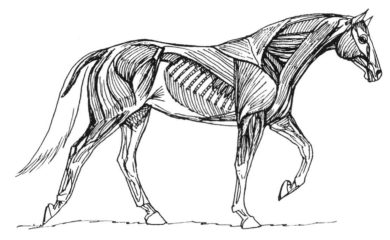

ANATOMY OF THE LOWER LEG

There are no muscles in the horse's lower leg below the knee and hock—only bones, tendons, ligaments, and some other structures. In order to know what a sound leg looks like, and to understand what can go wrong, it helps to know something about the anatomy of the lower leg.

The structures of the lower leg are the same in the front and hind legs below the knees (carpal joints) and hocks (tarsal joints). The structures of the lower legs provide support, flex and extend the joints, absorb shock, dampen vibration, and provide a rebound effect which helps each foot to leave the ground with less effort. The stay apparatus, a system of muscles, tendons, and ligaments at the front and back of each limb, allows the horse to lock his limbs and remain upright even while asleep. While the structures of the lower leg are primarily bones, ligaments, tendons, and the specialized structures of the foot, it is important to remember that the muscles of the upper leg are connected to the tendons of the lower leg and that the whole leg works as a coordinated limb.

Anatomy of the foreleg and hind leg.

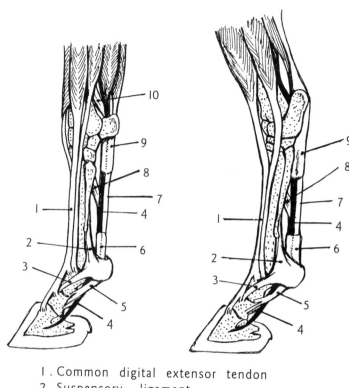

1. Common digital extensor tendon
2. Suspensory ligament
3. Lower branch of suspensory ligament
4. Deep digital flexor tendon
5. Lower branch of superficial flexor tendon
6. Lower tendon sheath
7. Superficial flexor tendon
8. Inferior check ligament
9. Upper tendon sheath
10. Superior check ligament

THE SUSPENSORY APPARATUS

The suspensory apparatus is a system of tendons and ligaments in the lower leg, which supports the fetlock joint. The suspensory apparatus carries most of the weight of the horse, especially at some phases of the stride. It prevents the fetlock joint from overextending or sinking too far toward the ground and helps absorb shock. The elastic structures of the suspensory apparatus also contribute to a rebound effect which helps the foot leave the ground at each stride.

The suspensory apparatus is similar in the front and hind legs. Structures of the suspensory apparatus are:

Suspensory Ligament: A large ligament that runs down the back of the cannon bone from the back of the knee (or hock) bones to the sesamoid bones, then separates into two lower branches which run diagonally forward on both sides of the pastern to join the common digital extensor tendon.

Other parts of the suspensory ligament system are a system of smaller ligaments which run down the sides and back of the fetlock joint and pastern bones to the coffin bone and navicular bone.

Collateral Ligaments: Ligaments that hold a joint together. They are present in pairs on the lateral (outer) and medial (inner) of each joint.

Inferior Check Ligament: Runs from the suspensory ligament at the back of the cannon bone to the deep digital flexor tendon, which it joins.

Deep Digital Flexor Tendon: Inner tendon, which runs from the forearm muscles down the back of the knee, around the fetlock joint, across the navicular bone, and fastens to the underside of the coffin bone.

Superficial Flexor Tendon: Outer tendon, which runs from the forearm muscles down the back of the knee, around the fetlock joint, and branches out to each side of the pastern.

Common Digital Extensor Tendon: Runs from the forearm muscles down the front of the leg to the top of the coffin bone.

Sesamoid Bones: Two small bones at the back of the fetlock joint that form a "pulley" through which the flexor tendons pass.

The suspensory apparatus is essential to the horse's ability to move and carry his weight, even at a standstill. Because the horse places so much weight on the suspensory ligaments, injuries to the structure can cause serious problems and are slow to heal because of the limited blood supply to ligaments.

THE STAY APPARATUS

The stay apparatus is a system of ligaments, tendons, and muscles which can lock the major joints of the front and hind legs and hold them firmly in position, so that the horse can remain standing even when relaxed. The suspensory apparatus is part of the stay apparatus and is the same in the front and hind legs. The upper part of the stay apparatus differs in the front and hind limbs.

Stay Apparatus of the Forelimb: Includes muscles which attach the forelimb to the ribs and neck, the muscles of the arm, elbow, and shoulder, the extensor and flexor muscles of the forearm and their tendons, and the suspensory apparatus of the lower leg.

Stay Apparatus (reciprocal system) of the Hind Limb: Includes the major muscles of the hindquarters (hip to stifle, thigh muscles, gluteals [croup muscles], and hamstrings), the ligaments of the stifle joint, and the tendons and ligaments of the gaskin, hock, and suspensory apparatus.

The hock and stifle are *reciprocal* joints, which means that when one bends or straightens, the other must also. The stifle joint is constructed so that the patella (kneecap) can be lifted and locked over the end of the femur (thigh bone) and held in place by the ligaments of the stifle joint. This locks the stifle and hock so that the horse can stand on the limb even when relaxed. The biceps femoris and quadriceps femoris muscles flex the stifle and unlock the patella.

ANATOMY OF THE FOOT

The foot has special structures to help it perform its essential functions: support, absorbing shock, traction for secure footing, and pumping blood back up through the lower leg.

Coffin Bone (Pedal Bone): Major bone of the foot; supports the weight of the horse.

Navicular Bone: Small wedge-shaped bone which lies under the back of the coffin bone.

Navicular Bursa: Fluid-filled sac which cushions the navicular bone and the deep flexor tendon.

Deep Digital Flexor Tendon: Crosses the navicular bone and attaches to the underside of the coffin bone.

Digital Cushion: Spongy structure, above the frog, containing blood vessels. Pressure on the digital cushion helps to pump blood back up the leg with each step.

Coronary Band: Outer band of tissue at the hairline, from which the hoof grows.

Corium: The deep tissue beneath the coronary band, which produces the horn.

Wall: The hard outer shell of the hoof, made of tiny hairlike tubules called insensitive laminae. The wall of the hoof supports the horse's weight. The wall angles backwards at each end, forming the bars. These aid in absorbing shock, allowing the foot to expand under pressure.

Sensitive Laminae: Tiny hairlike tubules which grow from the surface of the coffin bone and interlock with the insensitive laminae of the wall. The sensitive laminae have blood and nerve supply. The interlocking of these two types of laminae suspends the coffin bone in a strong, hard, protective casing, which can flex under pressure.

Periople: Thin, varnish-like outer layer of the hoof, which keeps moisture in.

Sole: The ground surface of the hoof, inside the wall. The outer layer of the sole is insensitive; the sensitive sole is the deep layer next to the underside of the coffin bone, which has blood and nerve supply. The sole should be arched, not flat. While it may touch the ground on soft ground, it is not a weight-bearing structure.

Anatomy of the foot.

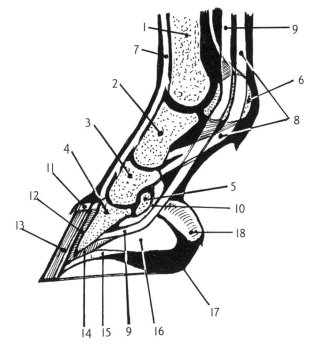

1. End of cannon bone
2. 1st phalanx (long pastern bone)
3. 2nd phalanx (short pastern bone)
4. 3rd phalanx (coffin or pedal bone)
5. Navicular bone
6. Sesamoid bone
7. Common digital extensor tendon
8. Superficial flexor tendon
9. Deep digital flexor tendon
10. Navicular bursa
11. Corium
12. Sensitive laminae
13. Insensitive laminae (wall)
14. Sensitive (inner) sole
15. Insensitive (outer) sole
16. Digital cushion
17. Frog
18. Lateral cartilage

Frog: A rubbery, wedge-shaped structure which lies between the bars. The frog helps to absorb shock and helps to pump blood back up the leg by compressing the digital cushion at each step.

Lateral Cartilages: Wing-shaped cartilages, which extend from the upper sides of the coffin bone and form the flexible bulbs of the heels. They aid in the expansion of the foot.

CONFORMATION

Conformation refers to the way a horse is built. Good conformation makes a horse attractive, but more important, good conformation is "functional": each part is built to work better. This makes a stronger, sounder horse that can move better.

There are different types of conformation that make some horses more suitable for certain jobs like cross-country riding and jumping, working cattle, or pulling heavy loads. The type of conformation that would make a good cow pony would not be suitable for an Olympic-level dressage horse. However, both horses could have good conformation for their own type. Some of the major conformation types include:

- *Sport horse type:* Horses suitable for dressage, jumping, or eventing, typically Thoroughbreds and warmbloods.

- *Hunter type:* Horses suitable for jumping and cross-country riding, typically Thoroughbreds and Thoroughbred crosses.

- *Stock type:* Horses suitable for western riding, performance events, or herding stock, such as Quarter Horses, Paints, and Appaloosas.

- *Saddle type:* Horses suitable for saddle seat, park, or gaited riding and fine harness, such as American Saddlebreds.

- *Pleasure and versatility type:* Horses suitable for a variety of uses, including English and western riding, dressage, driving, and general pleasure riding, such as Morgans, Arabians, and other breeds.

Each breed has its own conformation standard, which describes the conformation desirable for that breed. While good, functional conformation and soundness are important in any breed, there are certain typical breed characteristics which make a Morgan look like a Morgan or a Quarter Horse look like a Quarter Horse. These vary from breed to breed; for instance, a dished face is common and desirable in Arabians, while a straight profile is more common and preferred in Quarter Horses, and a Roman nose may be considered a correct and even noble profile for a Lipizzaner. Before you can evaluate horses of different breeds fairly, you must become familiar with many different breed standards and characteristics. In addition, remember that some breeds may produce horses of several different types. Information on breed standards and characteristics is available from the various breed associations.

Regardless of the breed of horse you like or the type of riding you do, some basic principles of conformation are always the same. These are the things that help make a horse sound, strong, and well balanced, and help him move well.

EVALUATING CONFORMATION

When evaluating a horse's conformation, look at the overall view first, from a distance. This lets you observe his balance, proportions, and angles. Next, look at him closely from each side, from the front, and from the rear. Evaluate the conformation of each part, noticing any blemishes or unsoundnesses, and compare each side with the other. This may help you notice a contracted foot, a swelling on one leg, or uneven muscular development. Finally, watch him move straight toward you, away from you, and from the side, to evaluate his movement.

Evaluating conformation is not simply a process of counting up faults. You must look at the horse's strengths as well as his weaknesses and decide which qualities, good as well as bad, are most important. Keep in mind the horse's breed and type and his suitability for the job he is intended to do.

IMPORTANT QUALITIES FOR FUNCTIONAL CONFORMATION

Good conformation is functional, which means that the horse is built to be stronger, sounder, and to do his job better. While individual conformation points are important, overall qualities such as balance, proportion, and the angles of major bones may have a greater effect on the horse's athletic ability than a single defect.

BALANCE

A horse with good conformation is built so that it is easy for him to move and carry a rider in good balance.

When you look at a horse from the side, he should have a well-balanced appearance. No part should look too large or too small for him, and all his parts should blend smoothly into each other. His legs should be in proportion to his body, not extremely long or short. His neck should appear long enough for good balance, and the head should not be too large.

A horse's body should appear fairly level from the neck back, so that his rump is not higher than his withers. If he is built low in front and high behind (called overbuilt or built downhill), he may carry more weight on his forehand than is normal. This makes it harder for him to move with good balance, especially under a rider, and puts extra stress on his front legs.

PROPORTIONS

A horse's proportions (size or length of each part in relation to each other) affect his ability to move. Some examples include:

- Long muscles move a limb farther than short muscles. Length in the neck, shoulder, forearm, croup, and from hip to hock helps a horse take longer strides for his size.

- Shorter is usually stronger. Short, wide, well-developed cannon bones and flexor tendons are stronger than long, narrow cannons. A horse with a long back may have springy gaits and greater scope over fences, but a long back is less able to carry weight and more prone to injury than a short back. Long pasterns are more prone to injury than shorter ones, and they put more stress on the flexor tendons.

Good proportions.

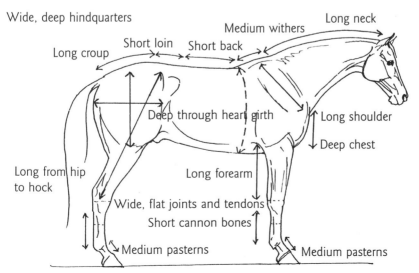

Wide, deep hindquarters
Long neck
Medium withers
Short loin   Short back
Long croup
Long from hip to hock
Deep through heart girth
Long shoulder
Deep chest
Long forearm
Wide, flat joints and tendons
Short cannon bones
Medium pasterns   Medium pasterns

- In the front legs, ideal proportions are a long shoulder, short arm, long forearm, short cannon, and medium pastern. This favors maximum length of stride, strength, efficiency, and range of motion. A short shoulder along with a long arm, short forearm, and long cannon causes a shorter, higher stride and is less strong.

- A long distance from hip to stifle (hocks well let down) indicates short, strong hind cannon bones and a more powerful hind leg.

ANGLES

The angles of the major bones affect the range of motion of the joints, the power and efficiency of the horse's stride, and his ability to absorb shock and give a smooth ride. Some important angles are:

Hind leg angles: The hind legs act as levers, which push the body forward and carry weight, especially during transitions and collection. Correct angles make these levers more efficient in pushing and carrying weight.

In the ideal hind leg, a vertical line dropped from the point of the croup runs down the back of the hock, cannon, and fetlock joint. This gives the hocks the best angle. If the hock angle is too acute (sickle hocks or standing under), they are placed too far under the body to push effectively, and this puts extra stress on structures at the back of the hock. If the hock joint angle is too open (straight hock), it swings forward and backward efficiently, but puts extra stress on the hock when carrying weight. If placed too far back, the hocks are less able to reach forward under the body, resulting in less engagement and power.

Shoulder angle: The shoulder blade rotates with each stride, swinging the entire foreleg forward and back. A sloping shoulder has more range of motion and can swing the foreleg farther forward, which is important for long strides and to bring the knees up in jumping. It also absorbs shock, which makes the gaits smoother. An upright (straight) shoulder cannot swing the leg as far forward or up, resulting in a shorter, rougher stride.

Angle of croup: The lumbosacral joint (the place where the loin ends and the croup begins) is important in balance and movement. The angle of the croup affects the horse's ability to flex this joint, tuck his hindquarters under him, and engage his hind legs for balance and power.

An ideal croup is long and slightly rounded, neither flat nor steep. This allows good angles, placement, and engagement of the hind legs. A very flat croup often goes with hind legs set too far behind the point of the buttock, which makes for poor engagement. A short, steep croup often goes with hind legs that "stand under" or have excessive hock angle (sickle hocks).

Shoulder and pastern angles.

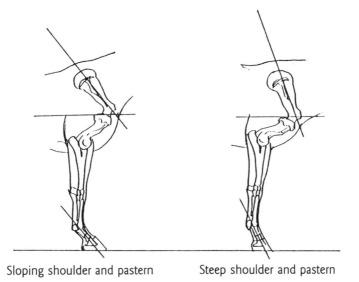

Sloping shoulder and pastern   Steep shoulder and pastern

Angle of croup and pelvis.

Normal angle of pelvis   Tipped pelvis   Hind leg too straight   Hind leg set too far
back; flat croup

Angle of pasterns: Pasterns should be of a medium angle, sloping enough to absorb shock, but not so sloping as to be easily injured or allow the back of the fetlock joint to strike the ground.

Angle of neck: The angle of the neck affects the way the horse naturally carries and uses his head and neck for balance. A low-set neck, which comes out of the front of the chest, results in a low head carriage and a tendency to move on the forehand. A neck set high with an upward angle ("swan neck") encourages flexibility and collection but makes it easy for the horse to carry his head too high and drop his back. The ideal neck depends on the type and purpose of the horse, but an average angle of neck is best for all-around balance and movement. (See diagram on page 18.)

TYPE OF MUSCLING

A horse's type of muscling affects his movement and way of going, and the kind of energy his muscles can deliver best. *Fast-twitch muscle fibers* deliver anaerobic energy for short but intense efforts; *slow-twitch fibers* deliver aerobic energy over a longer period. While all horses have both slow-twitch and fast-twitch muscle fibers, some have a preponderance of one type.

Horses with short, thick, bunchy muscles (such as sprinters, stock horses, and draft horses) tend to have a preponderance of fast-twitch fibers. They tend to move with shorter strides but with great power.

Horses with long, flat muscles (such as endurance horses) tend to have a preponderance of slow-twitch muscle fibers. They have long strides and efficient movement that can be sustained over longer distances.

Mid-range horses fall between the two extremes and are more versatile, having some ability to produce short, intense effort and some ability to carry a lower level of exertion over a distance.

For most breeds and types, middle-range muscling is preferred. When evaluating a horse, however, you should take into account the job he is bred and conformed to do. His type of muscling should be compatible with his purpose. His muscle tone and development reflect his current condition and training.

CONFORMATION AND SOUNDNESS

All good conformation is functional; that is, it helps the horse to be stronger, sounder, and perform better. However, some points (shown in the following illustration) are more directly related to strength and soundness:

- Straight legs (front and rear view).

- Legs correctly set.

- Correct angles of shoulder, pastern, and hock.

- Short, wide cannon bones with clean, well-developed tendons.

- Large, clean, flat joints (especially knees, hocks, and fetlock joints).

- Well-shaped feet, size in proportion to horse.

- Short, broad, and well-muscled back and loin.

- Symmetry (both sides and limbs appear even and equally developed).

POINTS OF GOOD AND POOR CONFORMATION

The horse's head and neck, the way he carries his head, and the movements and *balancing gestures* he makes with his head and neck are important to his balance and movement. His head and neck conformation affects his balance, the way he moves, and how easy he is to ride and train. The muscling of the neck is at least partly due to the way the horse is trained and ridden, and can change over time.

THE HEAD

The size of the head should be in proportion to the horse and to the length of his neck. The jaws should be wide enough to allow the horse to flex easily at the poll. The teeth should be correctly aligned (not parrot mouth or undershot jaw) so that the horse can graze and chew normally, and the nostrils should be large and flexible in order to take in adequate air when working hard. Large, prominent eyes with a kind expression are desirable; small, sunken eyes ("pig eyes") may make it harder for the horse to see all around him. Breed type, refinement, quality, and masculinity or femininity are expressed in the head and features.

Conformation faults of the head include: head too large (too small is less common), coarse head, narrow jaw, parrot mouth, and undershot jaw. Lesser faults include lack of breed type, or unattractive features such as pig eyes or lop ears.

Head, jaw, and throatlash conformation.

Parrot mouth

Undershot jaw (monkey mouth)

Good head and throatlash   Coarse head; thick throatlash

THE NECK

The neck should be of medium length, well muscled, and slightly arched, with a clean throatlash. It should blend smoothly into the withers and topline, and should come out of the top of the chest. Because the muscles of the neck help to move the forelegs forward, a long neck contributes to a longer stride. Certain breeds and types of horses may have characteristic muscling or higher or lower set necks, but a medium angle is best for all-around performance. A low-set neck, which comes out of the front of the chest, tends to make the horse move on the forehand. A high-set neck makes collection easier but may make it easier for the horse to raise his head too high and move with a hollow back.

Neck conformation.

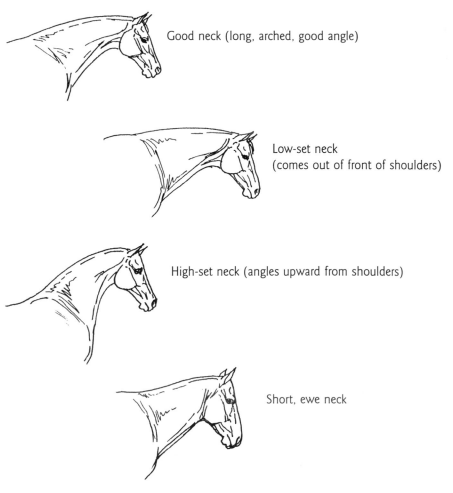

Good neck (long, arched, good angle)

Low-set neck
(comes out of front of shoulders)

High-set neck (angles upward from shoulders)

Short, ewe neck

Conformation faults of the neck include:

- *Short neck:* Too short a neck tends to shorten the stride and "scope," or jumping ability. A short neck often goes with a steep shoulder and long back.

- *Ewe neck:* A neck that is straight or hollow along the top and bulges at the bottom, it is often set at a sharp angle to the head and may be thick at the throatlash. This type of neck makes it difficult for the horse to flex easily at the poll, to go on the bit correctly, and to use his neck as a balancer.

- *Thick neck:* A thick neck is less flexible and makes the forehand heavier, which may affect the horse's balance and controllability. A horse with an excessively thick neck may be difficult to put on the bit correctly.

The Shoulders

The shoulders are important because they form the top of the front legs and the connection between the horse's forelegs and his neck and body. Good shoulders are long, sloping (at about a 50-degree angle), and clean but well muscled. Longer shoulder blades favor a longer stride. A more sloping shoulder has a greater range of motion than a straight or steep shoulder, resulting in a longer, smoother stride with more freedom of movement and better ability to bring the forelegs up in jumping.

Conformation faults of the shoulder include:

- *Short shoulders:* Shorter stride, less scope (jumping ability).

- *Straight or steep shoulder angle:* Shorter stride, less ability to bring the forelegs up in jumping, rougher movement with more concussion.

- *Heavy or "loaded" shoulder, too thick, heavily muscled, with thick neck:* Short, restricted stride and a heavy way of going; horse may "roll" from side to side as he moves.

Topline (Withers, Back, Loins, and Croup)

The topline includes the withers, back, loins, and croup. It includes both the skeletal structure and the muscles that lie over it. The muscling of the topline is an indicator of the way the horse has been trained and ridden, and can change over time.

The withers should be clean, prominent, and of medium height. The neck should blend smoothly into the withers, and the withers should blend smoothly into the back. Withers that are "well laid back" go with a sloping shoulder and good back conformation. Good withers help to hold a saddle in place and provide room for good muscling of the shoulders and back. Mutton withers (low withers hidden in fat) make saddle fitting difficult and are often associated with short shoulders. Very high withers make saddle fitting difficult.

The back should be short, moderately broad, and well muscled. It should blend smoothly into the withers, without a marked dip. A short, well-muscled back is stronger and carries weight better than a long back. A hollow back (sway back) is a fault which makes saddle fitting difficult; it also is weaker than a normal back and may make the horse move with poor engagement and a high head. A roach back is rounded upwards, especially at the loins; this tends to throw the saddle forward and makes balance difficult.

The loins should be short, broad, and well muscled; they should blend smoothly into the highest point of the croup. This creates a powerful coupling (the point where the loins end and the pelvis and sacrum begin). The coupling should be short and strong, with no more than a hand's space between the last rib and the point of the hip. A horse that is long in the loins, back, and coupling is usually less strong in the back and more prone to back injuries.

Conformation of body and topline.

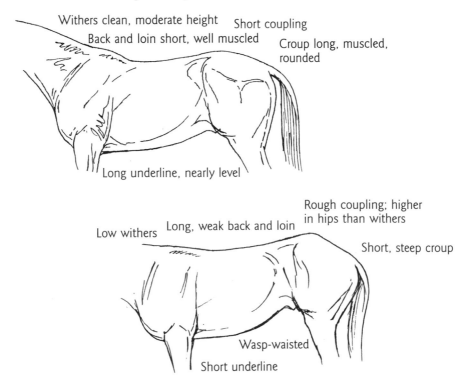

A rough coupling denotes a long, poorly muscled loin rising up to a bony, prominent peak; this is weak as well as unattractive. A jumper's bump is a prominent bulge at the highest point of the croup. This may be due to an extra prominent iliac crest (upper wing of the pelvis), which provides the attachment point for the powerful croup muscles and is often found on good jumpers. However, it can also be a swelling caused by an injury to the lumbosacral joint, especially when it is only on one side.

The croup is formed by the sacrum and the powerful gluteal muscles. It should be long, well muscled, and slightly rounded, with the tail set moderately high. Certain breeds and types may have a characteristically flatter or more rounded croup, and a higher or lower set tail.

A short croup has less powerful muscling than a longer croup, and a flat croup often goes with hind legs that are placed too far back, making engagement difficult. A steep croup (tipped pelvis) places the hind legs farther under the horse, and often goes with sickle hocks or incorrectly angulated hind legs. A short, steep croup ("goose rump") is weak and poorly angled.

Conformation of the croup.

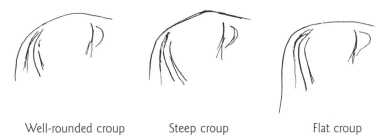

| Well-rounded croup | Steep croup | Flat croup |

The Chest, Body, and Underline

The chest, body, and underline are parts of the horse's torso; this area contains the lungs, heart, and vital organs. Good conformation of the body gives the horse better heart and lung capacity and is characteristic of an "easy keeper" that uses his food efficiently.

The chest should be deep and moderately wide, and the rib cage should be "well sprung," with well-arched ribs and a deep heart girth. This provides more heart and lung capacity for greater endurance, and also makes the horse better able to carry weight. The underline should be long and nearly level, which indicates good proportions and development.

Faults include: narrow chest, shallow heart girth, flat ribs, "wasp-waisted," pot belly, and short underline. The first four indicate lack of stamina and/or poor development. A short underline is the result of incorrect proportions, such as straight shoulders and a tipped pelvis.

THE HINDQUARTERS

The hindquarters are the horse's "motor"; good conformation is important for power and the ability to engage the hind legs for speed, power, and balance. Good hindquarters are wide and deep, with well-defined muscling which extends well down into the gaskins. When viewed from behind, the hindquarters should be evenly developed on both sides, well rounded over the croup, and wide and powerful through the stifles. The inner thigh and gaskin muscles should be as well developed as the outer muscles.

Faults include "rafter hips," which are weak, lacking muscle on the croup; "hip down," a condition in which the bony point of the hip has been fractured, leaving one hip bone lower than the other; and lack of muscle development in the stifle, inner thigh, or gaskin area. Fat, rounded hindquarters should not be mistaken for good muscling.

Hindquarter conformation (rear view).

 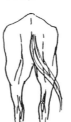 

Well-muscled,   Rafter hips;   Hip down
symmetrical   lack of muscling

THE FRONT LEGS

A horse's front legs carry more weight than his hind legs (about 55 percent of his weight when he is standing still). They do not pull him forward but reach out and carry his weight and absorb concussion (shock) at every stride. In order to do this well, the front legs must be set under the horse properly and must be strong, straight, and well developed.

GOOD FRONT LEG CONFORMATION, SIDE VIEW

When you look at the front leg from the side, a vertical line (called a plumb line) should drop straight down from the center of the shoulder blade, down the middle of the leg, to the fetlock joint. Half of the leg should be in front of the plumb line and half behind it.

FRONT LEG CONFORMATION FAULTS, SIDE VIEW

- *Standing under:* Most of the foreleg is behind the plumb line; the leg is too far back under the horse. This puts the horse's balance too far forward.

- *Camped out in front:* Most of the foreleg is in front of the plumb line; the leg is out in front of the horse. This puts more strain on the legs.

- *Over at the knee:* The knee is always slightly bent, which puts the lower leg too far back under the horse.

- *Back at the knee (calf knees):* The knee has a slight backward bend, with the cannon bone slanting forward. This puts extra stress on the flexor tendons and the fetlock joints and especially on the bones of the knee (carpal bones). It may lead to bone chips or fractures of the carpal bones when the horse is worked at speed, over fences, or when he is fatigued.

Foreleg conformation, side view.

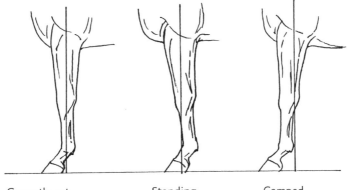

Correctly set foreleg   Standing under   Camped out in front

Foreleg conformation faults, side view.

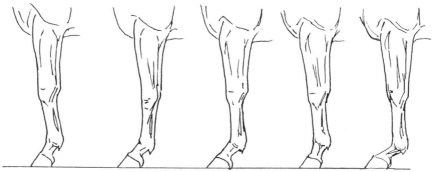

| Over at the knee (knee-sprung) | Back at the knee (calf knee) | Tied in below the knee | Short, steep pastern | Long, flat pastern |

GOOD FRONT LEG CONFORMATION, FRONTAL VIEW

The front legs should be straight and parallel, not too close together or too wide apart. This lines the bones up properly and makes each leg move straight. It also helps distribute concussion evenly as each foot hits the ground.

If you imagine a vertical line running straight down from the point of the shoulder, it should pass through the middle of the forearm, knee, cannon bone, fetlock joint, pastern, and foot.

FRONT LEG CONFORMATION FAULTS, FRONTAL VIEW

- *Base narrow:* The legs are closer together at the feet than they are at the chest, that is, inside the plumb lines. This conformation places the feet too close together, so it is easier for the horse to interfere (strike one leg with the other foot). It also puts more weight and concussion on the outsides of the feet and legs. Some base-narrow horses place one leg in front of the other as they walk, as if they were walking on a tightrope. This is called plaiting, or rope walking, and can lead to interfering or stumbling.

- *Base wide:* The legs are wider apart at the feet than they are at the chest, outside the plumb line. This conformation often goes with a narrow chest. It puts more weight and concussion on the insides of the feet and legs and may lead to ringbone.

Foreleg conformation, front view.

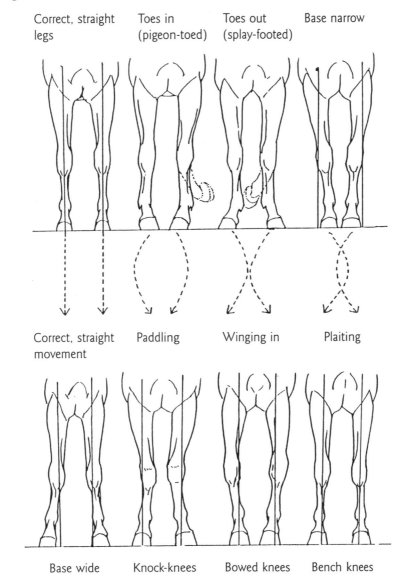

Correct, straight legs　　Toes in (pigeon-toed)　　Toes out (splay-footed)　　Base narrow

Correct, straight movement　　Paddling　　Winging in　　Plaiting

Base wide　　Knock-knees　　Bowed knees　　Bench knees

- *Knock-knees:* Knock-knees are knees that bend inward so that the knees are inside the plumb line. This puts extra stress on the knees and on the inside of the legs. Horses that are knock-kneed are prone to develop splints (see pages 50–52).

- *Bowed knees:* Bowed knees are knees that bend outward, so that the knees are outside the plumb line. This puts extra stress on the knees and on the outside of the legs. They are weaker than straight legs.

- *Bench knees (offset knees):* Bench knees are a conformation fault in which the cannon bones do not line up exactly with the center of the knees, but are set slightly to the outside. The outside of the knees get better support, and there is extra weight and stress on the inside of the lower leg. This often leads to splints on the inside of the cannon bone (see pages 50–52).

- *Toeing out (splay-footed):* The toes point out instead of straight ahead. This makes the foot swing in toward the opposite leg, a condition called winging in. This may lead to interfering and may cause lameness. It also causes uneven weight and concussion on the insides of the feet and legs, which may lead to ringbone.

- *Toeing in (pigeon-toed):* The toes point in instead of straight ahead. This makes the foot swing outward, which is called paddling. Paddling does not cause interference and is less likely to cause lameness than winging in, but it does put uneven weight and strain on the outsides of the feet and legs, which may lead to ringbone.

  Try walking with your toes pointed out, and notice how your legs swing in toward each other, making you "wing in" and perhaps "interfere." If you turn your toes in as you walk, you will find your legs swinging out, or "paddling." Remember, "Toes out causes winging in; toes in causes paddling."

HIND LEG CONFORMATION, SIDE VIEW

The horse gets his pushing power from his hind legs. The hind legs must reach forward under the horse's body (this is called engagement) at every stride, which provides the ground-covering pushing power. He also uses his hindquarters and hind legs to help balance himself in collected gaits and whenever he stops, turns, or makes transitions. Good hind leg conformation gives a horse more strength, power, and better balance.

When you look at the horse's hind legs from the side, his cannon bones should be vertical. A plumb line from the point of his buttock should run down the back of his hock and the back of his leg all the way to the fetlock joint. This gives the bones of his hind legs the best angles for strength and good movement.

HIND LEG FAULTS, SIDE VIEW

- *Camped out behind:* The hind leg is behind the plumb line from the point of the buttock. This makes it harder for the horse to engage his hind legs (reach forward). It is weaker than a correctly set leg.

Hind leg conformation and faults (side view).

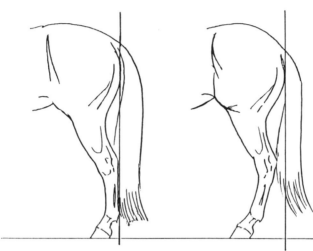

Correctly set hind leg (vertical line from point of buttock down back of hock and tendon)

Stands under behind (sickle hock)

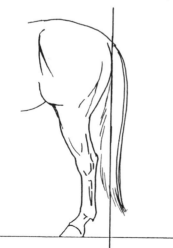

Post leg (straight hock and stifle)

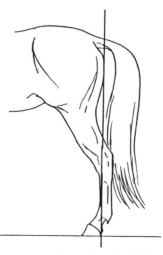

Camped out behind

- *Standing under (sickle hocks):* The hock is slightly bent (it has the shape of a farmer's sickle), and the hind legs are in front of the plumb line. This conformation puts the hind legs forward, under the horse, but it puts extra stress on the hocks. Horses with sickle hocks may develop problems such as curbs, thoroughpins, bog spavins, and bone spavins (see pages 58–60).

- *Leg too straight (post leg):* The hind leg is too straight in the hock and stifle joints; the whole leg is set in front of the plumb line from the point of the buttock. This makes it easy to swing the leg forward without bending it much. However, it puts more stress on the hind leg, especially the hock and the pastern. Straight hind legs are often seen in race horses.

Good Hind Leg Conformation, Rear View

The hind legs must be lined up properly, not too close or too wide, so that the horse can move straight. However, correct hind legs are not straight in quite the same way as the front legs. The stifles must point out a little so the horse can swing his hind legs forward without hitting his belly. The hocks and lower legs should be parallel and straight up and down, and the hind legs must not be too close or too wide apart.

Hind Leg Conformation Faults, Rear View

- *Cow hocks:* Cow hocks are hocks that point in toward each other, with the cannon bones slanting outward. This is a weakness which puts extra stress on the inside of the hocks and may lead to bone spavins, bog spavins, or thoroughpins (see pages 58–60).

- *Bowed hocks:* Bowed hocks are hocks that point outward, with the cannon bones slanting inward. They go with base-narrow conformation. Bowed hocks put extra stress on the hocks and on the outside of the foot and leg. This may lead to bog spavins or thoroughpins.

- *Too wide:* Hind legs that are placed too far apart may appear straight, but they go with base-wide conformation. They make it hard for the horse to reach well forward with his hind legs, which causes short strides.

- *Too narrow:* Hind legs that are too close together often lack good muscle development, which makes them weaker. They make it easy for a horse to interfere, which may cause injuries and lameness.

Hind leg conformation and faults (rear view).

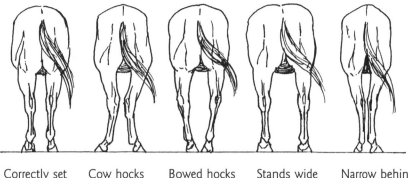

| Correctly set hind legs | Cow hocks | Bowed hocks | Stands wide behind | Narrow behind |

LOWER LEG AND JOINT CONFORMATION

The lower legs and joints should be "clean," which means that they are free from thickness or swelling and the bones, tendons, and other structures stand out clearly and are easy to see and feel.

The cannon bones should be fairly short, with clean, strong, and well-developed tendons. A horse with short cannon bones usually has stronger legs and often moves better.

The knees and hocks should be wide, flat, and clean, with clearly defined bones. Small, round joints are weaker and more easily injured.

The pasterns must have enough angle to absorb shock but must not be so long or so sloping that they are weak and easily injured. The front pasterns usually are a little more sloping than the hind pasterns.

LOWER LEG AND JOINT CONFORMATION FAULTS

- *Tendons tied in below the knee:* Tendons which are small, narrow, and poorly developed look "squeezed in" just below the knee, as if a band were tied around the horse's leg. This is a weakness, but don't confuse it with a bowed tendon, which is caused by an injury.

- *Pasterns too long and sloping:* Long, flat pasterns are weak and easily injured. They also put more stress on the tendons, which can contribute to bowed tendons (see page 52).

- *Pasterns too short and steep:* Short, upright pasterns do not absorb shock well. They cause rough gaits and transmit more concussion to the foot and the rest of the leg. This may contribute to concussion-related problems like ringbone, sidebone, and navicular disease. (see pages 55–57).

FOOT CONFORMATION

The horse's feet are especially important because they must carry the horse's weight and absorb shock with each step. When the horse steps down on his foot, it expands (grows wider), which helps to absorb shock; it contracts as the weight comes off the hoof. This pressure on the frog (and the cushion above it) helps pump blood through the hoof and back up the leg with every step. Good hoof conformation helps a horse to have strong, healthy feet and helps keep the horse sound.

The foot should be large and strong, with wide, well-developed heels and prominent bars. The frog should be large and should touch the ground (on soft ground), to promote good circulation and help the heels expand with each step. The sole should be arched, or concave (like a saucer turned upside down), not flat, and the horse's weight should be carried on the wall, not the sole. The walls should be strong and smooth, without cracks or rings.

FOOT CONFORMATION FAULTS

- *Too-small feet:* Too-small feet receive more concussion, especially to the navicular bone and coffin bone, since there is less area to absorb shock. They are more prone to develop navicular disease.

- *Contracted hoof (one hoof smaller than the other):* If one hoof is noticeably smaller than the other, it may indicate that the horse has been keeping most of his weight off that foot for a long period of time. This may be a sign of navicular disease or another long-term lameness of the foot.

- *Contracted heels:* The heel is very narrow; the frog is pinched in and small and does not touch the ground. Contracted heels can be caused by foot problems like navicular disease or by poor trimming and shoeing, and can be helped by good shoeing. However, narrow heels and a tendency toward contracted heels can be a conformation fault.

- *Flat soles:* Flat soles cause the weight to be carried on the sole instead of on the wall, which can make the feet tender. A "dropped sole" can be the result of laminitis, or founder, which causes the coffin bone to rotate and drop down.

- *Shelly feet:* Shelly feet have thin, brittle walls that crack and break off easily. This can make a horse's feet tender and can make it hard to keep shoes on him.

- *Foundered feet:* Foundered feet are feet which show damage caused by laminitis. The signs include dropped soles, separation of the wall from the sole at the toe, and irregular, wavy rings on the outside wall of the hoof. In severe cases, the horse may walk on his heels and his toes may grow abnormally long and curl upward. Founder usually makes the feet tender and may cause lameness or stumbling, depending on the severity of the damage and the condition of the horse's feet. Horses with foundered feet are prone to further attacks of laminitis and need careful management and therapeutic shoeing.

Foot conformation and defects.

Good conformation of foot with arched sole

Well-shaped front foot

Low heels

Contracted heels

Foundered foot

Clubfoot

- *Low heels:* Low heels may be a conformation fault, or they may be caused by excessive wear and neglect of foot trimming or poor horseshoeing practices. Low heels, especially when accompanied by long toes, place extra stress on the deep digital flexor tendon and on the navicular bone and bursa.

- *Clubfoot:* A clubfoot is a foot and pastern which are excessively upright (more than 60 degrees). The foot usually has high heels and a short toe. Some horses are able to move fairly well in spite of a clubfoot, but this condition will require special attention from the farrier. It is an inheritable defect, which makes it undesirable in a horse intended for breeding purposes.

CONFORMATION DEFECTS AND THEIR EFFECTS ON SOUNDNESS

No horse is perfect; most horses have some conformation defects, blemishes, or unsoundnesses. A conformation fault or defect is a structural problem, which may be hereditary. This makes horses with serious conformation faults poor candidates for breeding. Conformation defects are not unsoundnesses, nor do they always lead to unsoundness. However, serious conformation faults are undesirable because they make it harder for a horse to move and perform well, put more stress on certain parts, and make it more likely that injuries or unsoundnesses will occur, especially with hard work.

A blemish is an acquired defect, like a scar, which is unsightly but which does not affect the horse's usefulness. Some conditions (such as splints) may be classified as unsoundnesses when they are acute and cause lameness, but may subside, leaving only a blemish once they have healed.

Unsoundnesses are conditions or injuries which cause lameness or otherwise impair the horse's health or ability to work. Certain conformation defects may weaken a part and predispose a horse to unsoundness, but a conformation defect is not an unsoundness and does not always lead to unsoundness.

Conformation Defects and Their Effects

Conformation Defect	Effects	Associated Unsoundnesses
Base wide	More stress on inside of foot and leg.	Splints, ringbone
Base narrow	Causes plaiting, possible interference, or stumbling. More stress on outside of foot and leg.	Splints, ringbone
Toes in	Causes paddling. More stress on outside of foot.	Splints, ringbone
Toes out	Causes winging in, possible interference. More stress on inside of foot.	Splints, ringbone
Over at the knee	If severe, may cause stumbling.	Sometimes associated with contracted tendons.
Back at the knee (calf knees)	Extra stress on front of knee joint and flexor tendons.	Carpitis, carpal chip fractures
Bench knees	Uneven stress on splint and cannon bones.	Splints, ringbone
Knock knees	Uneven stress on splint and cannon bones and insides of feet.	Carpitis, splints, arthritis, ringbone
Standing under in front	Tends to move on forehand, front legs may be prone to stumbling.	
Camped out in front	Extra stress on flexor tendons and heels.	
Sickle hocks	Hock is less able to extend fully; more stress on plantar ligament.	Curb
Straight hock (post leg)	Hock is less able to flex and absorb shock, making collected gaits more difficult. Extra stress on hock joint.	Bone spavin, bog spavin, thoroughpin

continues

Conformation Defects and Their Effects (continued)

Conformation Defect	Effects	Associated Unsoundnesses
Hocks camped out behind	Horse is less able to engage hocks well under body, making collection difficult and giving less speed and power.	
Cow hocks	More stress on inside of hock and hind leg.	Bone spavin, bog spavin, thoroughpin
Bowed hocks	More stress on outside of hock and hind leg.	Bone spavin, bog spavin, thoroughpin
Straight stifle	Angle of stifle creates more stress on stifle joint, makes joint more prone to accidental locking.	Locked stifle, gonitis (inflammation of stifle joint)
Contracted heels	Lack of frog pressure causes poor circulation.	Associated with navicular disease
Flat soles	May be caused by coffin bone rotation due to founder; causes tender feet.	Sole bruises
Upright pasterns	Increased concussion.	Concussion-related ailments, such as navicular disease, sidebone, ringbone
Low heels	Increased stress on deep digital flexor tendon and navicular bone and bursa.	Bowed tendons, navicular disease
Long, sloping pasterns	Fetlock joint may "run down," striking the ground.	More stress on flexor tendons; sesamoiditis, bowed tendons
Straight shoulder	Less range of motion. Increased concussion in shoulder and foreleg, causing short stride and less ability to fold knees well in jumping.	
Mutton withers	Difficulty in fitting saddle and holding saddle in place. May be combined with other faults, such as short shoulder or being built downhill.	
High withers	Difficulty in fitting saddle; prone to wither sores and galls.	

Conformation Defect	Effects	Associated Unsoundnesses
Long back	Less ability to carry weight; more vulnerable to injury. However, may have more springy gaits and more scope over fences than short back.	
Short back	Prone to forging, especially if long legged.	
Slab-sided	Less room for heart and lungs; may lack endurance. Also, saddle may slip backwards.	
Flat croup	Often associated with hind legs set too far back (camped out behind), causing difficulty in engaging hind legs and in collection.	
Short, steep croup	Hindquarters less powerful because of less length of muscle. Often associated with tipped pelvis, sickle hocks, standing under behind.	
High in hips (overbuilt or built downhill)	Horse tends to move on the forehand; difficulty in balance and collection. Saddle may slip forward.	
Ewe neck	Causes difficulty in flexion and carriage of head and neck (often high headed).	
Short neck	Head and neck are less effective as a "balancer"; associated with short stride.	
Too-long neck (swan neck)	May be more difficult to ride on contact; tendency to raise or overflex neck and hollow the back.	Roaring is more common in large horses with very long necks.
Parrot mouth	Difficulty in grazing because upper incisor teeth extend out over lower teeth. If molars are also misaligned, may have difficulty in chewing feed.	
Undershot jaw	Lower incisors extend beyond upper incisors, making grazing difficult. If molars are also misaligned, may have difficulty in chewing feed.	

GAITS AND MOVEMENT

Horses are athletes; they are only useful because of their ability to move. Good movement is efficient, athletic, and easier to ride; it allows a horse to reach his full potential. Poor movement is ugly, difficult to ride, and uncomfortable and damaging to the horse.

Different breeds, types, and individual horses have different kinds of movement, which makes them more suitable for a particular purpose. Regardless of type, all horses share the same basic anatomy and principles of movement. Most horses perform the basic gaits: walk, trot, canter, and gallop (although certain breeds may perform specialized gaits). In addition, there are certain basic qualities which are essential to good movement and soundness in all horses.

Good movement is more efficient, safer, and easier for both horse and rider, and more beautiful than poor movement. When a horse moves well, his legs move straight, without swinging sideways or striking each other. He moves with good engagement (reaching well forward with his hind legs), which gives him power and good balance. His legs (especially his front legs) absorb shock or concussion so that he moves smoothly.

Good conformation makes it easier for a horse to move straight, with power and good balance, while poor conformation handicaps him in the way he moves.

THE HORSE'S BALANCE AND MOVEMENT

When he is standing still, about 55 percent of a horse's weight is carried on his front legs, and about 45 percent on his hind legs. His center of gravity is an imaginary balance point, located close to his heart girth line. However, a horse's balance during movement is dynamic rather than static. This means that his balance is constantly changing as he moves.

As a horse moves, his balance changes and his center of gravity moves. When he carries more weight on his forehand, his center of gravity shifts forward. When he tucks his hindquarters under him, he shifts his center of gravity and his balance backward.

Horse's center of gravity (at standstill).

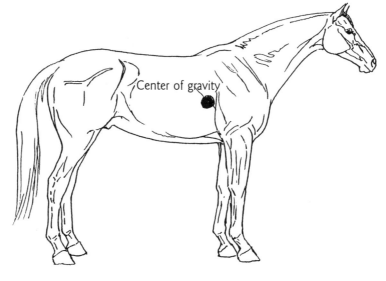

Center of gravity

Approximately 45% of weight
on hind legs

Approximately 55% of weight
on front legs

The horse's head and neck are especially important in changing his balance. When he carries his head forward and down, it moves his balance forward. When he raises his head and neck, it shifts his balance backward.

A horse is a "rear-engined" animal: his power comes from his hindquarters. At each stride, his hind legs reach forward, push against the ground and move him forward, and his front legs reach out and carry his weight.

THE PHASES OF A STRIDE

A stride is a sequence within a gait during which all four legs complete a step. Each leg completes the following cycle of movement:

- *Swing phase:* The leg swings backward, then flexes and swings forward.

- *Grounding (impact):* The hoof strikes the ground.

Good and poor engagement of hind legs.

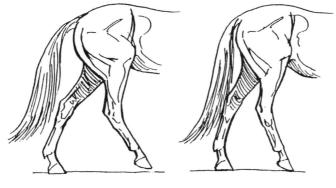

Good engagement: hind leg
reaches well forward

Poor engagement: short
stride, lacking reach

- *Support:* The leg bears weight.

- *Thrust:* Begins as the leg reaches a vertical position under the weight and continues until the foot breaks ground (breakover).

How a Horse Moves

When a horse moves, his hindquarter muscles provide the power that pushes him forward. The deep muscles of the back and spine stabilize the back and transmit the thrust to the rest of his body. The neck muscles aid the head and neck in acting as a balancer, and the muscles of the neck, shoulder, arm, and forearm move the forelegs and help to absorb shock. The abdominal muscles, along with deep inner muscles called the *psoas group*, draw the hindquarters and hind legs forward, engaging them under the body.

The Circle of Muscles

The entire system of muscle groups is called the "circle of muscles." In good movement, the circle of muscles works in harmony; each muscle group performs its function and is neither overstressed nor underused. Poor movement breaks up the smooth functioning of the circle of muscles and puts more stress on some muscle groups. This is less efficient, hampers the horse's athletic ability, and may eventually lead to soreness and unsoundness.

THE BASIC GAITS

The basic gaits of the horse are the walk, trot, canter, and gallop.

THE WALK

The walk is a four-beat gait, without suspension. An ordinary walk is approximately 4 miles per hour. The sequence of footfalls is left hind, left fore, right hind, right fore. A good walk is regular and ground-covering, with four evenly spaced beats and good engagement of the hind legs.

Faults in the walk include jigging, pacing (lateral walk), and a lazy, dragging walk.

The walk.

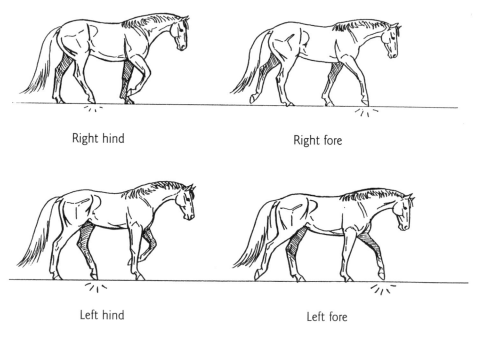

Right hind   Right fore

Left hind   Left fore

THE TROT

The trot is a two-beat gait in which the horse springs from one diagonal pair of legs to the other, with a moment of suspension between beats. The average speed of the trot is 6 to 8 miles per hour. The sequence of footfalls is left diagonal (left fore and right hind), suspension, right diagonal (right fore and left hind), suspension. A good trot is steady, balanced, and active, with an even rhythm and good engagement.

Faults in the trot include irregular trot, front foot landing first; irregular trot, hind leg landing first; short, stiff strides; loss of suspension; and a hurried, "running" trot.

The trot.

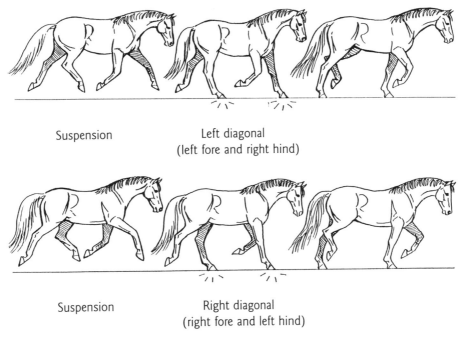

Suspension   Left diagonal
(left fore and right hind)

Suspension   Right diagonal
(right fore and left hind)

The Canter

The canter is a three-beat gait, with suspension, performed on either the right or left lead. The average speed of the canter is 8 to 10 miles per hour. The sequence of footfalls is *left lead*: right hind, diagonal pair (left hind and right fore), left fore, suspension; *right lead*: left hind, diagonal pair (right hind and left fore), right fore, suspension. A good canter is regular, balanced, slightly collected, and active, showing suspension or "jump" at every stride.

Faults in the canter include wrong lead, disunited canter (cross-canter), four-beat canter, lateral canter, and "flat" canter (lacking suspension).

The canter.

Left lead canter

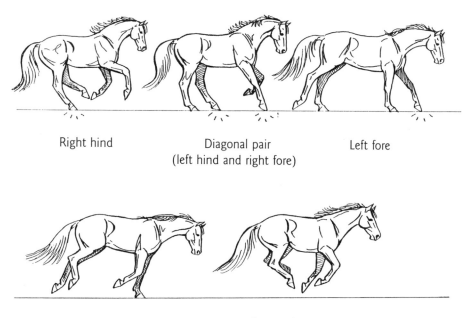

Right hind   Diagonal pair   Left fore
                       (left hind and right fore)

Suspension

THE GALLOP

The gallop is a four-beat gait with suspension; it is the horse's natural speed gait. The average speed of the hand gallop (controlled gallop) is 12 to 18 miles per hour; a racing gallop may exceed 35 miles per hour. The sequence of footfalls is *left lead*: right hind, left hind, right fore, left fore, suspension; *right lead*: left hind, right hind, left fore, right fore, suspension. A good gallop is steady and balanced, with long, sweeping strides and good engagement of the hind legs.

Faults in the gallop include wrong lead, disunited gallop, excessively high action ("climbing"), and poor balance ("strung out" or leaning on the forehand).

The gallop.

Left lead gallop

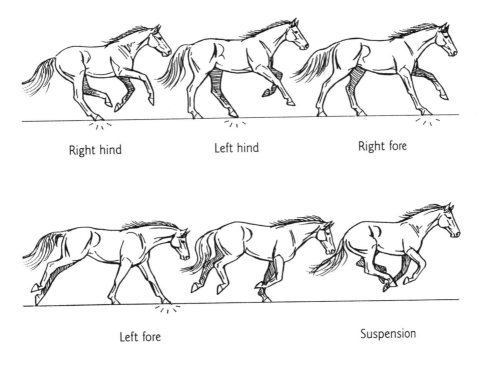

Right hind   Left hind   Right fore

Left fore   Suspension

EVALUATING MOVEMENT

When evaluating a horse's movement, watch him being led straight toward you and straight away from you at the walk and trot on a hard, level surface like a driveway. You should also view his movement from the side and watch him move in a circle at each gait in both directions or in a figure eight.

It is also helpful to see the horse work under saddle or on a longe line at a walk, trot, and canter on a longe line in both directions. When evaluating movement, you should note factors which may influence the way the horse moves, such as corrective shoeing, the way he is ridden or handled, and the footing.

GOOD MOVEMENT

Good movement depends on conformation and soundness and is affected by shoeing, footing, and by the way the horse is trained and ridden.

Normal and Faulty Movement	
Good, Normal Movement	*Faulty Movement*
Sound: free from lameness, pain or disability.	Lame, sore, or "off."
Symmetrical: both front and hind legs move evenly, with the same height, arc, and length of stride.	Asymmetrical, uneven, or unlevel; abnormal arc of stride.
Straight and true: when viewed from the front or rear, each foot travels straight, without deviating inward or outward.	Crooked: winging in, paddling, plaiting, interfering.
Free: the legs swing freely from the hip or shoulder.	Stiff, abnormally shortened strides.
Coordinated: steady, even, and well balanced.	Uncoordinated; unbalanced; stumbling.

MOVEMENT PROBLEMS

Certain conformation faults can lead to problems in the way a horse moves. All of these are less efficient than good, correct movement, and can also lead to injuries. Any movement problem can range from mild to severe. Special shoeing may help, so it is important to let your farrier know if your horse shows signs of any of the following movement problems:

LAMENESS

Lameness is a sign of pain or a serious problem in a leg. When a horse goes lame, it is important to determine which leg is lame and what is causing the problem. Diagnosing and treating lameness usually require help from your veterinarian.

To tell if a horse is lame, have someone lead him at a jog on a hard, level surface such as a driveway. The lead line should be loose so he can move his head up or down freely.

When a horse is lame, he favors his sore leg. He may stand with more weight on the good leg and rest the lame one (however, horses often rest one hind leg even when they are not lame.) When he moves, he tries not to step hard on the sore leg and usually takes a shorter step with that leg. If it is a front leg, he throws his head up as he steps on the sore leg, and down when he steps on the good leg. If it is a hind leg, he usually carries his hip higher on the lame side and throws his head down as the sore hind foot touches the ground. If a joint is sore, the horse may carry the lame leg stiffly and avoid bending it as much as usual. Sometimes you can hear that his hoofbeats are uneven; one may sound louder and one much quieter, like "CLIP, clop."

Identifying lameness.

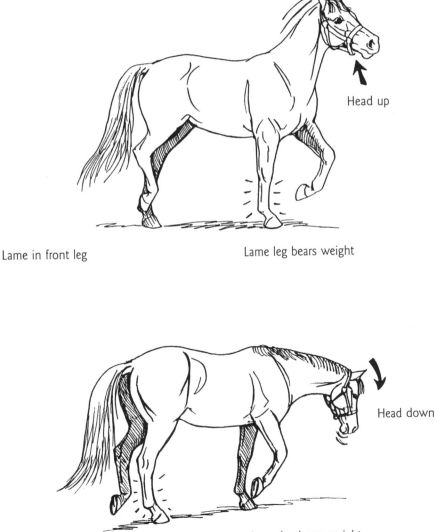

Head up

Lame in front leg

Lame leg bears weight

Head down

Lame in hind leg

Lame leg bears weight

STUMBLING

Stumbling can be a momentary accident, caused by poor footing or getting off balance, but a horse that often stumbles has a serious and dangerous movement problem. This can be caused by sore feet (especially navicular disease), arthritis, poor balance, or by neglecting shoeing or trimming and leaving the toes too long. Horses with sore heels may land on the toe, which may cause stumbling.

A horse that has a stumbling problem should be checked by a veterinarian and a farrier and should not be ridden until the problem has been evaluated and treated.

PADDLING

Paddling means that the horse's foot swings outward at each step. It is caused by toe-in conformation, which makes the foot break over at the outside of the toe. While paddling is usually less serious than other movement problems, the toe-in conformation associated with paddling causes uneven stress on the foot and lower leg, and can lead to outside (lateral) splints or ringbone.

WINGING IN

Winging in means that the horse's foot swings inward at each step. It is caused by toe-out conformation, which makes the foot break over at the inside at each step. Winging in may lead to interfering. The toe-out conformation associated with winging in also causes uneven stress on the foot and leg, which may lead to inside (medial) splints or ringbone.

INTERFERING

Interfering means striking one leg against the other during movement. This can cause cuts or bruises, especially if the interfering foot is shod. It can also contribute to splints, especially in young horses.

Interfering is commonly caused by toe-out conformation, which causes the legs to wing in during movement. When a horse's legs are too close together or base narrow, he is more likely to interfere. Even a horse with good, straight legs may interfere when doing lateral work or being longed, which is why protective boots or bandages are recommended for this kind of work. Interfering tends to get worse when the horse is tired (for instance, at the end of a long trail ride).

Horses that interfere may be helped by special shoeing or trimming, or they may need to wear boots to protect their legs.

PLAITING

Plaiting, or "rope walking," means placing one leg in front of the other as the horse moves. This can lead to interfering or stumbling. It is caused by base-narrow conformation. Corrective shoeing may help, but the horse may need to wear boots to protect his legs.

Faulty movement (front view).

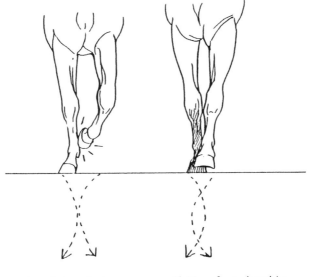

Interfering: foot
strikes opposite leg

Plaiting: foot placed in
front of opposite leg

FORGING

When a horse forges, he hits the heel of his front foot with the toe of his hind foot, usually at the trot. This causes a clicking sound. Forging is more common when a horse is tired or moving too much on his forehand, and when his toes are too long. It also can occur in a horse that has a very short back and long legs. Young horses that have not yet learned to move in balance under a rider are apt to forge, especially when trotting too fast.

A good farrier can help a horse that forges with special trimming or shoeing. Riding in good balance can also help.

OVERREACHING

When a horse overreaches, the toe of his hind foot "grabs" the heel of his front foot, inflicting an injury. A horse can pull a shoe off when overreaching if his hind toe catches the heel of the shoe. A high overreach occurs when the hind foot hits higher up, on the pastern or the tendon; this can inflict a serious injury. Overreaching most often happens when galloping or jumping, or playing in deep or muddy footing. The sticky footing holds the front foot just long enough for the oncoming hind foot to catch it. The same things that cause forging (short back and long legs, long toes, moving on the forehand, fatigue) can also contribute to overreaching.

Bell boots may be used to protect a horse's heels from overreaches when he must work or be turned out in deep or muddy footing. Protective boots (galloping boots) or exercise bandages are used to protect against high overreaches. Good shoeing can also help.

Faulty movement (side view).

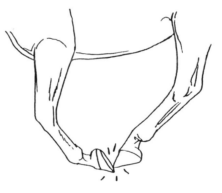

Forging: toe of hind foot strikes sole or heel of front foot

Overreaching: toe of hind foot "grabs" front heel, inflicting injury

CHAPTER 4

SOUNDNESS, BLEMISHES, AND UNSOUNDNESSES

A sound horse is one without any physical problems or defects which interfere with his health or his ability to do his work. In order to be considered sound, a horse must not be lame, blind in one or both eyes, or have a pulmonary (heart or lung) defect that would affect his ability to work.

An unsoundness is a physical problem than makes a horse lame or unable to do his job. An unsoundness is worse than a blemish (like a lump or a scar), which may be unsightly but doesn't keep him from being able to work. Certain conditions may be considered unsoundnesses while they are acute and cause lameness, but may subside, leaving a blemish. (Some examples are curbs, splints, and bucked shins.) Whether a particular condition is considered an unsoundness or a blemish depends on whether it causes lameness or affects the horse's ability to work. Conformation defects are not unsoundnesses, but they can contribute to certain unsoundnesses by making one part weaker or putting it under more stress. Because conformation is inheritable, horses that have unsoundnesses associated with conformation defects are poor prospects for breeding.

Some unsoundnesses are caused by an injury like a fall or a blow, while others develop slowly. Some are more serious than others or get worse over time. Others might make a horse unable to do strenuous work, like racing, hunting, or eventing, but may not bother him if he does easier work. You should recognize common unsoundnesses and know what causes them. Always have your veterinarian do a prepurchase examination, to avoid buying an unsound horse.

LEG AILMENTS

CAPPED ELBOW, CAPPED HOCK

Inflammation of the bursa over the elbow or hock—due to pressure or bruising over a long period of time—results in a capped elbow or hock. A capped elbow or hock eventually results in a permanent swelling and blemish, but does not usually cause lameness. A capped elbow (shoe boil) is usually caused by the pressure of the heel of the horse's shoe against the elbow when lying down. A capped hock may be caused by kicking the stall or trailer, or by lying on a hard floor with insufficient bedding.

Swellings.

Capped elbow   Capped hock   Windpuffs   Bog spavin   Thoroughpin
(shoe boil)   (windgalls)

CARPITIS

Carpitis is inflammation of the knee, or carpal joint, caused by stress or trauma. It is most common in racehorses and horses with calf knees. The knee becomes hot, tender, and swollen, and the horse tends to move his foreleg in a sideways arc in order to avoid bending the painful joint. Severe cases may involve fractures of the bones of the knee or small chips of bone within the joint. Carpitis may subside with rest and proper treatment, or joint surgery may be required. It is an unsoundness.

SPLINTS

Splints are hard lumps that appear between the splint bones and the cannon bones. The splint bones must support some of the horse's weight, yet they do not have a bone underneath them for support. They are attached to the cannon bone by a small ligament, which gradually hardens as the horse matures. If the

Splints.

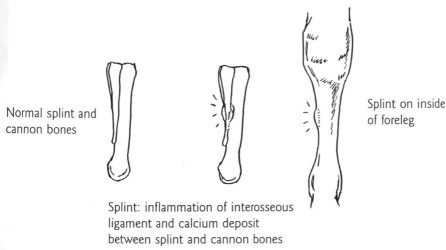

Normal splint and
cannon bones

Splint: inflammation of interosseous
ligament and calcium deposit
between splint and cannon bones

Splint on inside
of foreleg

A splint is usually hot and painful when it first happens. With rest, it usually becomes "quiet" and does not cause any further lameness if it is allowed to heal completely. If it does not cause lameness, an old healed splint is usually considered a blemish, not an unsoundness.

BOWED TENDONS

A bowed tendon happens when a tendon is stretched too far, often because of a slip or an accident when the horse is overtired. Some of the tendon fibers are torn, and as they heal, scar tissue forms, creating a thickening or "bow" in the tendon. It may be a "high bow" or a "low bow," depending on whether it is high up, close to the knee, or low down, close to the fetlock joint.

Conformation problems which put extra stress on the tendons (such as calf knees, long sloping pasterns, long toes and low heels, or weak, tied-in tendons) make horses more prone to bow a tendon. However, any horse can bow a tendon through an accident like a slip or a fall. Fatigue and lack of fitness are common factors in tendon injuries.

When a bowed tendon first happens, it is extremely painful, and the horse will be very lame. After it heals, the horse may not be lame, but the leg may never be quite as strong as it was before. A bowed tendon is usually considered an unsoundness.

Front leg ailments.

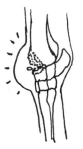

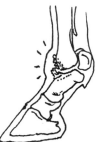

Osselet: ar[
front of fetl

Carpitis: arthritis in carpal joint

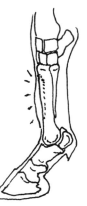

Bucked shin: periostitis, or infl:
of periosteum (bone covering)
of cannon bone

splint bone or the ligament are injured (by excessive concussion
struck), or if they are required to carry more than their share of wei
may happen if the horse has bench knees), this ligament may tear
inflamed. The body tries to heal and strengthen the ligament by bu
calcium deposit (a "splint") to weld the splint bone to the cannon l
the inflammation is over, the horse is usually sound. However, if t
deposit interferes with the suspensory ligament, it may cause lamene
splint would then be considered an unsoundness.

Splints are usually seen in young horses that are just starting to do
Carrying a heavy weight, striking one leg against the other, worki
circles, jumping, and working on hard ground all can lead to splints
in horses under five years old or those with bench knees or crooked l
a good reason to wait until young horses are mature before working t

Bowed tendon.

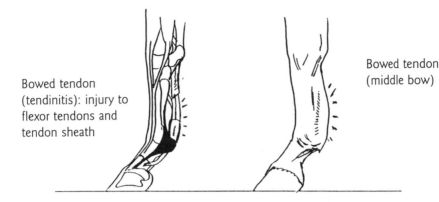

Bowed tendon
(tendinitis): injury to
flexor tendons and
tendon sheath

Bowed tendon
(middle bow)

BUCKED SHINS

Bucked shins are an inflammation of the periosteum (bone covering), sometimes with micro-fractures, on the front of the cannon bones, usually in the front legs. The shin becomes hot and very sore, and the horse is lame. It is common in young racehorses, especially when worked fast over hard ground. The lameness subsides with rest and proper treatment.

A slight enlargement on the front surface of the cannon bones may be left after the inflammation has subsided. This condition is usually considered a blemish.

OSSELETS

An osselet is arthritis of the fetlock joint and is usually found in the front legs, resulting in calcium deposits (exostoses) around the front surface and edges of the joint. It produces an enlarged fetlock joint with a "square" appearance and a reduced range of motion. The fetlock joint is hot, swollen, and inflamed, and the horse is quite lame; the inflammation may subside with rest and proper treatment. Osselets are most common in racehorses; they are considered an unsoundness.

SUSPENSORY LIGAMENT INJURY

A suspensory ligament injury is a sprain caused by trauma, resulting in tearing and damage to the fibers of the suspensory ligament. The seriousness of the unsoundness depends on which part of the suspensory ligament is injured and the severity of the injury. Suspensory ligament injuries take a long time to heal because the horse carries so much weight on the suspensory ligament, and it is easily reinjured. Sometimes the injury is serious enough to end a horse's jumping career, or even leave him permanently unsound.

FOOT AND PASTERN AILMENTS

CONTRACTED HEELS

Contracted heels are not necessarily an unsoundness, because they do not cause lameness, but they often are seen as part of an unsoundness such as navicular disease. The heels and frog become narrow and fold in upon themselves, and the frog does not touch the ground. Contracted heels are caused by lack of frog pressure; as the foot becomes more contracted, there is less frog pressure, which worsens the condition. As the frog folds in on itself, thrush may develop.

Contracted heels are often seen in navicular disease, because the horse tries to keep his weight off his painful heels. They are also seen in horses that have gone without exercise for long periods and have been confined to stalls. The condition can result from neglected hoof trimming or poor shoeing. Some horses have naturally deep, narrow heels; they may be more prone to develop contracted heels.

CORNS

A corn is a bruise on the ground surface of the hoof, in the angle between the bars and the wall. They are caused by pressure of the shoe in the wrong place, especially when a shoe is left on too long and overgrown, or if a shoe is fitted too small. A suppurating corn is a corn that has become infected and developed a pus pocket.

Corns cause lameness and therefore are considered an unsoundness, but they are usually easily treated with good shoeing.

HOOF CRACKS AND DEFECTS

Hoof cracks range from superficial blemishes to serious unsoundnesses. The depth of the crack (especially if it extends into the sensitive laminae) and if it causes lameness determine whether it is considered a blemish or an unsoundness. Most hoof cracks can be treated easily by proper hoof trimming or shoeing if they are caught early.

Sand cracks: May run up from the ground surface or downward from the coronary band. They are usually caused by concussion, especially in unshod horses whose feet have been allowed to grow too long, flare, and split. Dry, hard feet and dry ground conditions may contribute to the problem. Sand cracks are classified as toe cracks, quarter cracks, or heel cracks, depending on their location on the hoof wall.

Hoof wall defects: A deep cut or injury to the coronary band may leave a scar which interrupts the normal growth of the hoof wall. This may cause a chronic crack or hoof wall defect, or simply a large scar which extends to the ground surface. Most such defects are blemishes, but a severe defect that causes lameness would be considered an unsoundness.

Hoof cracks.

Toe cracks   Quarter crack   Heel crack   Scar in coronary band, causing defect in hoof wall

FOUNDER (CHRONIC LAMINITIS)

Founder refers to damage to the structures of the hoof as a result of laminitis. During an attack of laminitis, the normal circulation within the hoof is disturbed and the sensitive laminae begin to separate from the insensitive laminae of the hoof wall. The coffin bone begins to tear loose from its attachment to the hoof wall, and the toe of the coffin bone rotates downward. In severe cases, the coffin bone may sink under the weight of the horse until it comes through the sole. Acute laminitis is extremely painful; the horse will be reluctant to move or even stand up, and lameness is severe.

After the acute laminitis is over, the horse may still suffer from the effects of the damage that it caused. His feet may exhibit irregular growth rings (founder rings) caused by the disturbance in his circulation, and his toes may grow abnormally long and may turn upwards. He may have dropped soles; the sole of the foot is flat, sensitive, and loses its concave arch. There may be separation of the white line (a gap between the outer wall and the inner laminae), which is prone to infection (seedy toe). The horse may move with a short, "pottery" gait, as if moving on eggs, and may set his feet down heel first. Depending on the degree of damage, a horse with chronic founder may or may not be lame, but he will need special shoeing and extra attention from the farrier. Founder is considered a serious unsoundness.

NAVICULAR DISEASE

Navicular disease is a problem deep within the foot. The deep flexor tendon passes down under the navicular bone and fastens to the underside of the coffin bone. The navicular bursa is a soft pad which protects the bone where the tendon crosses over it. The deep flexor tendon presses against the navicular bone and navicular bursa with every step.

Foot ailments.

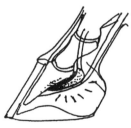

Founder (damage due to laminitis):
rotation of coffin bone,
dropped sole,
separation of wall at toe,
irregular rings on hoof wall.

Navicular disease: inflammation of navicular
bone, bursa, and deep digital flexor tendon.
Navicular bone degenerates; tendon may
develop bone spurs.

Corn: bruise located in angle between
wall and bar; may develop abscess
(suppurating corn).

Contracted heels: heels narrow;
frog recedes.

Navicular disease occurs when the navicular bursa (the pad), the navicular bone, or the end of the tendon becomes inflamed and sore. It usually starts out as a mild lameness that comes and goes, and may disappear when the horse is warmed up. Later, as the bone and tendon become inflamed and roughened, the lameness may become severe and the horse may be lame all the time. Because the pain is in his heels, the horse will try to walk on his toes, which gives him a short, "tiptoe" gait and may make him stumble. Navicular disease is a serious unsoundness.

Navicular disease is most common in middle-aged horses whose conformation promotes concussion. Small feet, narrow heels, upright pasterns, and long toes with low heels can all contribute to navicular disease. The right kind of shoeing and medication may offer some relief.

RINGBONE

Ringbone occurs in the pastern area. It is an *exostosis* (calcification, or bony lump) on the pastern bones. If the ringbone is away from the joints (called non-articular ringbone), the horse may go sound after a period of rest. "High ring-bone" is arthritis (inflammation and calcification) in the pastern joint, between the two pastern bones. Eventually the bones may fuse, or grow together, and the horse may go sound. "Low ringbone" occurs at the coffin joint, between the end of the pastern bone and the coffin bone; it lies inside the hoof, so it cannot be seen without x-rays. This type of ringbone is usually more serious, and the horse usually becomes permanently lame. Ringbone is considered an unsoundness.

Ringbone.

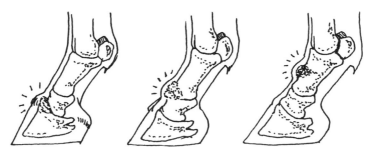

Low ringbone: arthritis and calcium deposits in coffin joint

High ringbone: arthritis and calcium deposits in pastern joint

Non-articular ringbone: calcium deposit on pastern bone, not located at a joint

Excessive concussion contributes to ringbone, and it is more common in horses with very upright pasterns. It may also occur in horses that carry extra weight on one side of the foot and leg because of crooked legs.

SIDEBONE

Sidebone occurs when the collateral cartilages of the coffin bone (which are shaped like wings and form the bulbs of the heel) turn to bone. This happens gradually and usually does not cause lameness unless the sidebones become very large or one gets broken. You can feel the collateral cartilages by pressing just above the bulbs of your horse's heel and on the sides of his foot, just above the coronary band. In a young horse, they will feel springy (like the cartilage of your nose). When they have calcified or turned to sidebones, they will feel hard.

Large sidebones and sidebone problems are more common in large, heavy horses with big feet, especially if they have straight pasterns which cause more concussion. Sidebone is usually not considered an unsoundness unless it causes lameness.

Sidebone.

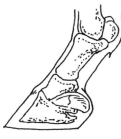
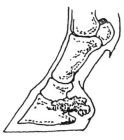

Normal lateral cartilage   Sidebone: lateral cartilage becomes calcified

HIND LEG AILMENTS

The hind legs do not have to handle as much concussion as the front legs do, so concussion problems like ringbone, navicular disease, and sidebone are not as common in the hind legs as they are in the front legs. However, the hind legs must push powerfully, especially in collected gaits, jumping, going up and down hills, and when working in deep footing. Hind leg problems are more likely to be caused by strain than by concussion.

Hock ailments.

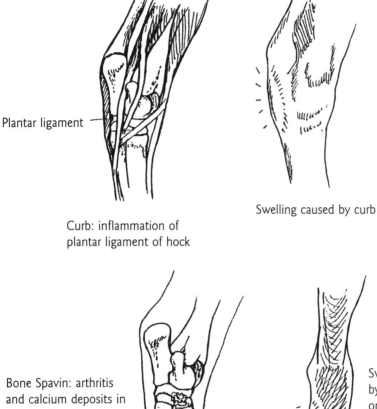

Plantar ligament —

Curb: inflammation of
plantar ligament of hock

Swelling caused by curb

Bone Spavin: arthritis
and calcium deposits in
bones of hock

Swelling caused
by bone spavin
on lower inside
of hock

CURB

A curb is a sprain of the plantar ligament, which runs down the back of the hock. This causes a thickening of the ligament at the lower end of the hock joint. It is caused by extra strain on the back of the hock, and usually causes lameness. Because it is an injury to a ligament, a curb can take a long time to heal. A curb is considered an unsoundness if it causes lameness; after it heals, it is considered a blemish.

Curbs are often associated with sickle hocks or horses that "stand under" in the hind legs. This conformation fault makes the hock weaker and puts more strain on the ligament.

Bone Spavin

A bone spavin (also called a jack spavin) is arthritis in the small bones of the hock. When the bones of the hock are irritated by stress or concussion, they may form bone spurs (calcium deposits) on the edges of the bone. These are painful and cause lameness. The lower bones of the hock fit closely, like saucers stacked on top of each other; there is not much movement between them. If the calcium deposits eventually cause these bones to fuse together, there is no more pain and the horse may become sound again. However, if arthritis or calcium deposits occur in the upper part of the hock joint, the hock will not be able to move normally and the horse may become permanently lame.

A bone spavin usually produces a hard swelling low down on the inside of the hock joint. It is considered an unsoundness.

Bone spavin is more common in horses that put extra strain on their hocks. Cow hocks, bowed hocks, and very straight hocks are more prone to develop bone spavin.

Bog Spavin

A bog spavin is a soft swelling on the front of the hock. It is usually cool, not hot or painful, and seldom causes lameness. A bog spavin usually occurs when a horse's hocks have been under some stress, but not enough to make him lame. This causes the joint to produce too much synovial fluid, resulting in a soft swelling. After a while, the joint capsule becomes enlarged and is always full of fluid, forming a bog spavin. A bog spavin usually gets smaller when a horse is rested and may be larger after he has worked hard.

Bog spavins are often seen in horses that have very straight hocks or in horses with weak hock conformation that do work that is hard on their hocks. A bog spavin is usually considered a blemish, not an unsoundness, but it is a sign that the horse's hocks have been under stress.

Thoroughpin

A thoroughpin is usually caused by stress or strain on a weak hock, especially in a horse with sickle hocks. The tendon sheath produces extra fluid, which stretches it, causing a soft, cool swelling in the upper part of the hock. Like a bog spavin, it is a sign of stress but doesn't usually cause lameness. If it doesn't cause lameness, a thoroughpin is considered a blemish.